MAY 24 1980

FEB 6 1981

FEB 25 1981

MAR 1 8 19

JUN 1 8 1

JUL 1 6 19

FEB 24 1

MAR 1

JUL 14

JUL 14

FEB 18

MAR 6

SEP 4

SEP 18

OCT 2

OCT 16

JUL 30

FEB 21

PRINTED IN U.S.A.

HIGHSMITH 42-312

J 1803

J 03851

RENEWAL

04966

RENEWAL

RENEWAL

RENEWAL

J 3530

08207

D1159137

ABE LINCOLN,
Make It Right!

By Dorothy Fay Richards

Illustrated by John Nelson

THE CHILD'S WORLD

ELGIN, ILLINOIS 60120

23930

Library of Congress Cataloging in Publication Data

Richards, Dorothy Fay, 1915-
   Abe Lincoln, make it right!

   SUMMARY: Relates four incidents in the life of
Abraham Lincoln prior to his term as president.
   1. Lincoln, Abraham, Pres. U.S., 1809-1865—
Juvenile literature. 2. Presidents—United States—
Biography—Juvenile literature. [1. Lincoln,
Abraham, Pres. U.S., 1809-1865. 2. Presidents]
I. Nelson, John, 1928- II. Title.
E457.905.R5   973.7′092′4   [B]   [92]   78-7690
ISBN 0-89565-033-9

Distributed by Childrens Press, 1224 West Van Buren Street, Chicago,
Illinois 60607.

There was a road to New Salem, but it was just two wheel tracks. On this hot September morning, a little old lady walked toward town. She was carrying her sunbonnet. She wanted to feel a breeze through her hair.

She passed Robert Johnson's place. She looked to see if he was working. Sometimes he was making wheels. Sometimes he was making furniture. Today, she could not see him. But she could hear his plane smoothing a piece of wood.

She passed Peter Lukin's cabin. He made his hammer go rat-a-tat-tat as he worked on a child's shoe.

"Howdy, Luke."

"Howdy, Miss Hildie."

Miss Hildie passed Josh Miller's blacksmith shop. At the shop, Josh was often busy with red-hot iron. It was heavy work, shaping iron into horseshoes. But this morning, Josh was standing out front.

"Howdy, Josh."

"Howdy, Miss Hildie."

A crowd of people had gathered at Samuel Hill's woolen mill. What had happened? People were talking all at once, loudly. Some were shoving and pushing a big animal.

Oh, Miss Hildie saw what had happened. One of the oxen that turned the big wheel of the machine had fallen. But soon he was up and working again.

The neighbors greeted the little old lady. They shared with her the news of the village. They told her who was sick and who was well. They told her who was away and who had come home. They told her who was new-born and who had died. And they told her who was getting married.

Miss Hildie went into the town's new store, Offutt's. The store was only one month old. After a while, she came out with a small package and turned to go home.

Ann Rutledge saw her from the door of her parents' place and called out, "Better stay to dinner, Miss Hildie. We're going to have beans and potatoes and bacon. And we've got plenty."

"Thank'ee kindly, Ann, but I must get back."

Slowly, Miss Hildie made her way back through the little village. She followed the road out of town. Soon she was out of sight.

After noon, the little village was quiet. No oxen fell. The hours went by slowly. Nobody came or went. Only the bees were noisy in the honeysuckle vines on Rutledge's fence.

Through the open door of Offutt's store, there was one sign of life to be seen. It was the wiggling of a big toe. It moved slowly back and forth, back and forth.

The owner of the toe was lying on the counter. He had his head on a grain bag, reading. One leg was crossed over the other.

This was not Denton Offutt, the owner of the store. This was Abe Lincoln, his helper.

Abe Lincoln was not lazy. He just liked to read. If there was no one in the store and no work to do, Abe read. Sometimes he read stretched out on the counter — all long arms and legs with sharp elbows and knees like a grasshopper. Other times, he read lying in the shade of the oak tree in the yard.

Once he was seen stretched over a wood pile. That did not look one bit comfortable! And when he was plowing, he read at the end of each row. This gave the horse time to catch an extra breath or two.

Abe turned a page. He was reading about a law case, and he wanted to see how it all turned out.

Suddenly, Abe sat up! When that little old lady had bought the tea, how much had she asked for? A half pound? Abe looked at his scales. The weight on one side said, "Four ounces."

Uh-oh! There should have been an eight-ounce weight on that side! He had given that lady only half the tea she paid for!

Abe got to his feet. He weighed four ounces of tea.
He wrapped it carefully. Then he called out to Mr. Offutt, "Mind the store! I won't be back till after dark!"

Abe wouldn't finish the book he had been reading
until later. He had a long walk ahead of him.

Ann Rutledge was drawing water at the well. She
called out, "Be back in time for supper, Abe?"

"Not tonight," was the answer.

Abe heard a dog barking as he passed the school
house. Its lonely sound carried all the way to Purka-
pile Creek. It made Abe think of his own dog. He
thought of the time his dog was left behind . . .

the time Abe had jumped into the icy river to go and get the dog and bring him along. That was when Abe had been helping his father and family move, the winter before.

As Abe walked, he thought about other things. Mostly, he thought about making things right.

One good thing about making a mistake . . . you could almost always make it right.

Abe thought about when he was a little boy. It made him smile to think about it. His kind step-mother had teased him about growing so fast. Indeed, he was tall for his age.

"Abe," she had said, "I declare! It's a good thing your hair is clean or you would ruin my ceiling!"

So, while she was gone one day, Abe asked a small friend to muddy his feet. Then Abe held him upside down. He had the boy make muddy footprints across the ceiling.

When Mrs. Lincoln saw what the two boys had done, she put her hands on her hips and laughed and laughed. And so did Abe. Then she said, "Now, Abe, make it right!" Of course, he had meant to anyway. He got the bucket of whitewash. Then he made the ceiling fresh and new again.

Then there was the time Abe had to work for two days. He pulled dried cornstalks out of the fields. That was to pay Joshua Crawford for the book Abe had ruined. Abe certainly hadn't meant to get that book rained on. But it had happened, and it was his job to pay for it.

The shadows along the road grew longer. The sun began to sink lower, behind the trees. Abe kept thinking about the past. Sometimes, Abe thought, sometimes things seemed as if they never would work out right.

Abe shook his head as he remembered how long he had dreamed of being free. Abe had wanted to be his own master. He had wanted to earn his own money and buy the things he needed. Instead, he had stayed at home to help his father. He had given his father every cent he earned until he was 21.

For a while Abe had worked on a flatboat. He had even wanted to become a steamboat captain.

But his father had said, "No, Abe. I need you."
And that was that.

Then, even after Abe was 21, he had stayed at home for another year, helping. He had split three thousand rails with a friend. These were used to fence in his father's land.

Indeed, Abe Lincoln was a hard worker. No one could keep up with him at harvest time.

Abe had walked a long way by now. It was past sun-setting. The whip-poor-wills were whistling. It was a lonely sound. So Abe began to whistle "Jimmy Crack Corn," just to keep himself company.

Abe began to think of other ways to make things right. Sometimes it wasn't trying to fix a mistake. Sometimes it wasn't doing extra good work. Sometimes it was trying to help others.

One freezing day, Abe had seen his friend Ab Trent. Ab was a small fellow. Ab had been out in the snow with rags on his feet. He had been chopping away with his ax.

"What are you doing, Ab? Where are your shoes?"

"Got none. Earning money for some, now."

So Abe had sent Ab to the store to get warm. Then
he had cut the wood for Ab. And he had received the
dollar for pay.

"The wood is cut," he had told Ab. "Here is your
dollar. Go buy those shoes before you work again."

As Abe walked along, he thought about how he had gotten into the habit of giving talks. He spoke about many things. He knew lots of stories that showed people the right thing to do.

Once, he had been trying to tell a crowd a good idea for using their river, the Sangamon. In back of the crowd he had seen a man picking on a friend of his. So he had fixed it,

and then finished his speech.

Thinking about it, Abe grinned, and whistled "Jimmy Crack Corn" some more.

At last! There was the cabin. A thin bit of smoke was curling from the chimney.

Abe called out, "Hal-looo there! Anybody home?"

Miss Hildie came to the door and looked into the shadows.

Miss Hildie knew only one person that tall and thin. "Why, Abe Lincoln, is that you? I just saw you in town! What did you walk out all this way for?"

"To give you this," said Abe, taking off his old battered hat. He handed her the neatly-wrapped package of tea. He had carried it on his head, inside the hat.

"I weighed it wrong," he said. "I gave you only four ounces. I should have given you eight."

"Land-a-mighty! Whoever would think you would go to so much trouble for that! You could have given it to me next time I was in your store!"

"You don't come that often. I might not have been there. Better to make it right, right now."

"Well, I never! Abe Lincoln, you do make things right! Won't you come in for supper before you walk back again? I've got mush and milk, both fresh. And I have cornbread. Now what could be better?"

Abe Lincoln was glad to stay.

Before long, Denton Offutt's store failed. Later, Abe Lincoln opened a store with a man named William Berry. That store failed, too. It owed a lot of money. Mr. Lincoln and Mr. Berry sold it. But the men who bought it failed and walked away. Soon after that, Mr. Berry died. Mr. Lincoln decided he would pay back every cent that was owed. And he did. But it took him many years.

To earn the money, he worked as an extra "hand." He worked for anyone who needed help. He helped with harvest and he

split rails.

He worked as a blacksmith. He was a clerk in a store. He took care of a mill. He did plowing. He even kept money records and wrote letters for people. He became a postmaster, then a surveyor.

By this time, many people knew and trusted Abraham Lincoln. When he ran for public office, they elected him. They knew if this man saw something wrong, he would make it right.

When he was not busy with the law-makers, Mr. Lincoln studied law. Finally, he became a lawyer.

One time, he spoke to some young men. They were thinking of becoming lawyers.

"Don't take a case . . . . unless you think it is right. If the man who has come to you for help is wrong, show him what to do to make the problem right. . . . If you cannot be an honest lawyer . . . be honest without being a lawyer!"

Mr. Lincoln became the 16th President of the United States. We remember him most for righting the wrong of slavery.

IN THIS TEMPLE
AS IN THE HEARTS OF THE PEOPLE
FOR WHOM HE SAVED THE UNION
THE MEMORY OF ABRAHAM LINCOLN
IS ENSHRINED FOREVER